COLLEC
ANODISED CAP BADGES

This book is dedicated to three dear friends
Lulu, Ben and Freya

COLLECTING
ANODISED CAP BADGES

Peter Taylor

LEO COOPER

First published in 1998 by
LEO COOPER
an imprint of
Pen & Sword Books Limited
47 Church Street, Barnsley, South Yorkshire S70 2AS

Copyright © Peter Taylor, 1998

ISBN 0 85052 637 X

A CIP catalogue of this book is available
from the British Library

Printed by Redwood Books Limited
Trowbridge, Wiltshire

*For up-to-date information on other titles produced under the Leo Cooper imprint,
please telephone or write to:*

Pen & Sword Books Ltd, FREEPOST, 47 Church Street
Barnsley, South Yorkshire S70 2AS
Telephone 01226 734222

Contents

Foreword

When I first started collecting military badges and buttons, back in the 1940's there were few books dealing specifically with the subject, indeed only a couple of very slim paperbacks published in the early years of the war, and scattered reference to badges or buttons in various other books.

With the result that I, like other collectors of the period, built up our own records and exchanged information on our researches with each other. If today's collectors can imagine their hobby without Kipling-King, Gaylor, Parkyn, Westlake, Ripley, Cox, Wilkinson, Westlake & Churchill and the many editions of Edwards, as well as magazines which cover the subject in one form or another, they may begin to understand why I for one always welcome any book which helps plug some of the gaps which still exist in our knowledge of the subject.

When anodised badges and buttons first appeared a few years after World War II ended, I think it is true to say, they were not very popular with the majority of collectors. Most of us felt that we already had plenty to go at without adding a new category to the field. At this time of course, it was quite common to collect the Empire as a whole, and apart from the new designs which appeared amongst the anodised issues, other items tended to be ignored. This was unfortunate, as many of the early issues are now very difficult to find, and reliable information is hard to come by.

In recent years, many collectors have turned to collecting just anodised items. There are, I think two reasons for this.

Firstly they regard it as a nice compact field, which offers the chance of completeness, no matter how remote, which is rather more than can be said of practically any other field of military badge or button collecting, no matter how limited a field one collects in. Secondly is the realisation that there is an ever growing number of reproductions and fakes appearing on the market, and collectors in general are under the impression that the anodised field of collecting has escaped the attentions of the individuals who pedal this type of rubbish.

Unfortunately this is not quite true, as reproduction anodised badges have appeared in recent years, but hopefully this book will provide some guidance to collectors and possibly help them to avoid the disappointment which always follows when one realises too late that last acquisition is of doubtful origin.

Walter Lambert
1998

Introduction

This book is devoted to the collecting of anodised cap badges. Anodised badges first appeared in 1948 with the introduction of new battle and service dress. The Army clothing department asked the badge manufacturers to come up with a metal that did not need polishing and would stay bright and clean. It was intended to make it easier for the enlisted men to keep their badges and buttons luminous and in good condition.

The first badge to be produced in the new anodised aluminium and to be shown to the clothing department was that of the 6th Dragoon Guards. This badge appears with a slider, lugs and a single lug in the middle so it can be fitted on a waist belt clasp. The badge is quite crudely made and is rare as only 7 are known to exist.

The Army started trials of the new badge in 1948; the first unit to receive the new cap badges was the Royal Army Ordnance Corps (illustration 251); only 3 of these have ever been found. By 1949 other Corps and Infantry Regiments received their new aluminium badges. Some of the early King's Crown badges are extremely rare, for example the Glider Pilot Regiment (illustration 276); only 2 have ever been found - one in a collection in England and the other in a collection in Canada. In 1953 the crown changed to Elizabeth's Crown which again led to some rare badges being discovered, for example; the Glider Pilot Regiment (illustration 277), 12th Royal Lancers (illustration 19) and East Yorkshire Regiment (illustration 142).

When you start collecting anodised cap badges, it is best to try and get the pre-1968 badges as these tend to be the rarest and more expensive badges. Since 1968 a lot of amalgamations have taken place and some regiments disappeared altogether such as York & Lancaster Regiment, the Buffs (East Kent), Lancashire Fusiliers etc.

After 1968 the new brigade system was introduced. These badges are fairly common with the exception of 2: the East Anglian Brigade and the Yorkshire Brigade. With the Yorkshire Brigade you have to make sure it is not the Yorkshire Volunteers which came in to being in the seventies.

By the 1990's the new amalgamations came into existence i.e. The Light Dragoons (illustration 33) And the Royal Dragoon Guards (illustration 35).

I have tried to include all the known badge makers names and where possible, have added the dates when the patterns were sealed.

Badge collecting is an enjoyable and relatively inexpensive pastime.

Acknowledgements

I would like to thank the following people; Michael Jones for his research, drawings and the use of his collection; Gerry Parsons for his original drawings for the book; Rick Butterfield, John Gaylor, Hugh King, Walter Lambert for their help, knowledge and inspiration; Crown Imperial Society for the use of their journals; Cheryl Jackson for typing the first draught; and finally, to my wife, Christine for checking it all.

Further Reading

Head Dress Badges of the British Army by Kipling & King
      (Volume 2)
Military Badge Collecting by John Gaylor
Regimental Badges by Major T.J. Edwards
Badges & Insignia of the British Armed Services
      by May, Carman & Tanner
Crown Imperial Society Journals

ANODISED BADGE MAKERS

1	J.R.GAUNT	LONDON
2	J.R.GAUNT	LONDON LTD
3	J.R.GAUNT	B'HAM
4	FIRMIN	LONDON
5	FIRMIN & SONS	LONDON
6	DOWLER	BIRMINGHAM
7	Wm DOWLER	(B'HAM)
8	GROVE M.F.G.	B'HAM
9	MARPLES & BEASLEY	BIRMINGHAM
10	LONDON BADGE & BUTTON Co LTD	
11	LB & B	
12	R.A.HUGHES LTD	
13	SMITH & WRIGHT LTD	
14	H.W.TIMINGS	BIRMINGHAM
15	TOYE, KENNING & SPENCER LTD	
16	TKS	
17	T & S	
18	G.S.TYE & Co	BIRMINGHAM

1. THE LIFE GUARDS
QC. ALL GOLD

37 mm HIGH

2. THE BLUES AND ROYALS
QC. ALL GOLD

3. THE ROYAL HORSE GUARDS
(The Blues)
QC.

43 mm HIGH

4. THE HOUSEHOLD CAVALRY
QC. ALL GOLD

38 mm HIGH

5. 1st THE QUEEN'S DRAGOON GUARDS
(There are three versions of this badge)
ALL SILVER

43 mm HIGH

6. THE QUEEN'S BAYS
(2nd D.G.)
QC. ALL GOLD

7. 6th DRAGOON GUARDS
Trial pattern only
KC. GOLD & SILVER

38 mm HIGH

8. 3rd CARABINIERS (P.O.W.'S D.GDS)
SILVER & GOLD

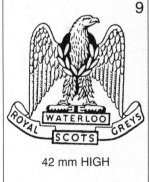

42 mm HIGH

9. ROYAL SCOTS GREYS
(There are three versions of this badge.
Different wing design etc.)
ALL SILVER & GOLD

10

WATERLOO

ROYAL SCOTS DRAGOON GUARDS

48 mm HIGH

10. ROYAL SCOTS DRAGOON GUARDS
SILVER & GOLD

11

11. ROYAL SCOTS DRAGOON GUARDS BAND
ALL GOLD

12

45 mm HIGH

12. 4th/7th ROYAL DRAGOON GUARDS
(Also one collar size worn by NCO's)
BOTH ALL SILVER

13

38 mm HIGH

**13. THE ROYAL DRAGOONS
(1st DRAGOONS)**
GOLD & SILVER

14

28 mm HIGH

14. 5th ROYAL INNISKILLING DRAGOON GUARDS
ALL SILVER

15

3RD THE KING'S OWN HUSSARS

33 mm HIGH

15. 3rd THE KING'S OWN HUSSARS
SILVER & GOLD

16

7TH QUEEN'S OWN HUSSARS

45 mm HIGH

16. 7th QUEEN'S OWN HUSSARS
QC. GOLD & SILVER

17

THE QUEEN'S OWN HUSSARS

33 mm HIGH

17. THE QUEEN'S OWN HUSSARS
SILVER & GOLD

18

LANCERS

40 mm HIGH

18. 9th QUEEN'S ROYAL LANCERS
QC. ALL SILVER

19

43 mm HIGH

19. 12th ROYAL LANCERS
QC. GOLD & SILVER

20

40 mm HIGH

20. 9th/12th ROYAL LANCERS
QC. SILVER & GOLD

21

21. QUEEN'S ROYAL IRISH HUSSARS
QC. SILVER & GOLD

22

40 mm HIGH

2. QUEEN'S ROYAL IRISH HUSSARS
QC. SILVER & GOLD

23

38 mm HIGH

23. 10th ROYAL HUSSARS
(There are two versions of this badge.
Different design to plumes.)
BOTH SILVER & GOLD

24

41 mm HIGH

24. 11th HUSSARS
(There are three versions of this badge.)
ALL GOLD

25

41 mm HIGH

25. THE ROYAL HUSSARS
SILVER & GOLD

26

30 mm HIGH

26. 13th/18th ROYAL HUSSARS
QC. ALL GOLD

27

35 mm HIGH

27. 14th/20th KING'S HUSSARS
BLACK & GOLD, ALSO ALL GOLD, ALSO ONE
WITH HEAD FACING RIGHT. BLK & GOLD

11

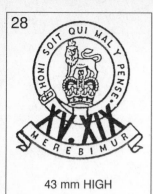

28

43 mm HIGH

28. 15th/19th THE KING'S ROYAL HUSSARS
QC. GOLD SILVER

29

43 mm HIGH

29. 16th/5th QUEEN'S ROYAL LANCERS
QC. SILVER & GOLD

30

42 mm HIGH

30. 17th/21st LANCERS
ALL SILVER, ALL BLACK, ALSO THIS IS THE NEW QUEEN'S ROYAL LANCERS. ALL SILVER

31

48 mm HIGH

31. ROYAL ARMOURED CORPS
QC. ALL SILVER

32

43 mm HIGH

32. ROYAL TANK REGIMENT
QC. ALL BLACK
QC. ALL SILVER

33

45 mm HIGH

33. THE LIGHT DRAGOONS
(There are two versions of this badge)
QC. SILVER & GOLD
QC. SILVER & GOLD & BLUE

34

48 mm HIGH

34. KING'S ROYAL HUSSARS
(This badge has F.R. on it's breast)
BLACK & GOLD

35

43 mm HIGH

35. ROYAL DRAGOON GUARDS
(43mm x 43mm)
ALL SILVER
ALSO ONE SILVER/RED/BLK

36

30 mm HIGH

36. ROYAL DRAGOON GUARDS
(3cm x 3cm)
Worn by NCO's
ALL SILVER

37

45 mm HIGH

37. THE AYRSHIRE YEOMANRY
(Earl of Carrick's Own)
There are two versions of this badge, one with large 'of' and one with small 'of.') ALL GOLD

38

40 mm HIGH

38. BERKSHIRE AND WESTMINSTER DRAGOONS
GOLD & SILVER

39

28 mm HIGH

39. THE BERKSHIRE YEOMANRY
ALL GOLD
ALSO IN ALL SILVER

40

BERKSHIRE

40. THE BERKSHIRE YEOMANRY
(Beret)
ALL GOLD

41

41. ROYAL BUCKINGHAMSHIRE HUSSARS
(Scroll inscribed Royal Bucks Hussars)
QC. ALL SILVER

42

40 mm HIGH

42. ROYAL BUCKINGHAMSHIRE HUSSARS
(Circlet inscribed the Buckinghamshire Regiment)
QC. SILVER & GOLD

43

40 mm HIGH

43. THE CHESHIRE YEOMANRY
(Earl of Chester's)
SILVER & GOLD

44

44. THE NORTHUMBERLAND HUSSARS
KC. ALL SILVER

45

45 mm HIGH

45. THE NORTHUMBERLAND HUSSARS
QC. ALL SILVER

46

46. ROYAL DEVON YEOMANRY
ARTILLERY
KC.

47

40 mm HIGH

47. ROYAL DEVON YEOMANRY
ARTILLERY
QC. ALL GOLD

48

40 mm HIGH

48. ROYAL DEVON YEOMANRY
QC. ALL SILVER

49

49. THE ESSEX YEOMANRY
(Beret)
KC. ALL GOLD

50

47 mm HIGH

50. THE ESSEX YEOMANRY
(47mm x 30mm)
QC. ALL GOLD

51

32 mm HIGH

51. THE ESSEX YEOMANRY
(Beret)
QC. ALL GOLD

52

52. THE SURREY YEOMANRY
(Queen Mary's Regiment)
QC. ALL SILVER

53

40 mm HIGH

53. THE SURREY YEOMANRY
(Queen Mary's Regiment)
As 52 but smaller
QC. ALL SILVER

54

43 mm HIGH

54. THE QUEEN'S OWN YORKSHIRE
YEOMANRY
QC. ALL SILVER

55

56

40 mm HIGH

57

45 mm HIGH

55. THE SHROPSHIRE YEOMANRY
KC. ALL GOLD

56. THE SHROPSHIRE YEOMANRY
QC. ALL GOLD

57. QUEEN'S OWN MERCIAN YEOMANRY
QC. SILVER & GOLD

58

59

60

40 mm HIGH

38 mm HIGH

58. THE SHERWOOD RANGERS YEOMANRY
Strap inscribed Notts Sherwood Rangers Yeomanry)
QC. ALL GOLD

59. THE SHERWOOD RANGERS YEOMANRY
(Circlet inscribed Sherwood Rangers Yeomanry)
QC. ALL GOLD

60. THE SHERWOOD RANGERS YEOMANRY
(Circlet inscribed the Sherwood Rangers Yeomanry)
QC. ALL GOLD

61

62

63

45 mm HIGH

45 mm HIGH

35 mm HIGH

61. THE SUSSEX YEOMANRY
KC. ALL GOLD

62. THE SUSSEX YEOMANRY
QC. ALL GOLD

63. LEICESTERSHIRE & DERBYSHIRE YEOMANRY
(Prince Albert's Own)
QC. GOLD & SILVER

64. THE NORFOLK YEOMANRY
(The King's Own Royal Regiment)
QC. ALL GOLD

45 mm HIGH

65. LOYAL SUFFOLK HUSSARS
GOLD & SILVER

66. LOYAL SUFFOLK HUSSARS
(Beret)
ALL GOLD

38 mm HIGH

**67. SUFFOLK & NORFOLK
YEOMANRY**
QC. SILVER & GOLD

68. THE STAFFORDSHIRE YEOMANRY
(Queen's Own Royal Regiment)
KC. ALL SILVER

42 mm HIGH

69. THE STAFFORDSHIRE YEOMANRY
(Queen's Own Royal Regiment)
QC. ALL SILVER

**70. QUEEN'S OWN WORCESTERSHIRE
HUSSARS**
KC.

**71. QUEEN'S OWN YORKSHIRE
DRAGOONS**
KC.

**72. Q.O. OXFORDSHIRE
HUSSARS**
KC.

73

73. QUEEN'S OWN ROYAL GLASGOW YEOMANRY
QC.

74

74. THE SCOTTISH HORSE
KC.

75

75. THE LOTHIAN & BORDER HORSE

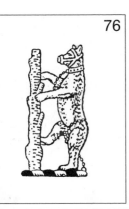

76

76. THE WARWICKSHIRE YEOMANRY

77

35 mm HIGH

77. QUEEN'S OWN WARWICKSHIRE & WORCESTERSHIRE YEOMANRY
GOLD & SILVER

78

40 mm HIGH

78. ROYAL GLOUCESTERSHIRE HUSSARS
ALL GOLD

79

42 mm HIGH

79. NORTH IRISH HORSE
QC. All SILVER

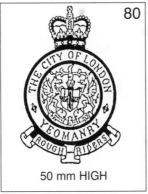

80

50 mm HIGH

80. THE CITY OF LONDON YEOMANRY
(Rough Riders)
QC. GOLD & SILVER

81

45 mm HIGH

81. THE KENT & COUNTY OF LONDON YEOMANRY
(Sharpshooters)
QC. GOLD & SILVER

82

40 mm HIGH

82. DENBIGHSHIRE YEOMANRY
(Scroll inscribed Caernarvon & Denbigh Yeo)
SILVER & GOLD

83

83. DENBIGHSHIRE YEOMANRY
(Scroll inscribed Flint & Denbigh Yeo)
SILVER & GOLD

84

38 mm HIGH

84. ROYAL WILTSHIRE YEOMANRY
(Prince of Wales's Own)
SILVER & GOLD

85

85. PEMBROKE YEOMANRY
(Castlemartin)
GOLD & SILVER

86

34 mm HIGH

86. PEMBROKE YEOMANRY
(Castlemartin)
(Beret)
GOLD & SILVER

87

45 mm HIGH

87. SOUTH NOTTINGHAMSHIRE HUSSARS
ALL SILVER

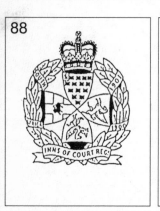

88

88. THE INNS OF COURT REGIMENT
QC. ALL GOLD

89

40 mm HIGH

89. INNS OF COURT & CITY YEOMANRY
QC. GOLD & SILVER

90

35 mm HIGH

90. 1st COUNTY OF LONDON YEOMANRY
(Middlesex, Duke of Cambridge's Hussars)
QC. SILVER & GOLD

18

91. HERTFORDSHIRE YEOMANRY
QC. ALL SILVER

92. HERTFORDSHIRE & BEDFORDSHIRE YEOMANRY
ALL GOLD
ALSO ALL SILVER

45 mm HIGH

93. THE HIGHLAND YEOMANRY
QC. ALL SILVER

35 mm HIGH

94. QUEEN'S OWN LOWLAND YEOMANRY
SILVER & GOLD

45 mm HIGH

95. Q.O. DORSET & WEST SOMERSET YEOMANRY
QC. SILVER & GOLD

96. THE LEICESTERSHIRE YEOMANRY
(Prince Albert's Own)
ALL GOLD

40 mm HIGH

97. THE DUKE OF LANCASTER'S OWN YEOMANRY
(there are two versions of this badge, a one part badge & a two part badge)

98. THE EAST RIDING YEOMANRY

99. HAMPSHIRE CARABINIERS YEOMANRY
KC.

100

48 mm HIGH

100. THE FIFE & FORFAR YEOMANRY
ALL SILVER

101

25 mm HIGH

101. QUEEN'S OWN YEOMANRY
GOLD & SILVER

102

40 mm HIGH

102. NORTH SOMERSET & BRISTOL YEOMANRY
QC. ALL SILVER

103

103. THE LOVAT SCOUTS
(One found with square lettering to motto, one
found with tall lettering to motto)
ALL PATTERNS - ALL SILVER

104

50 mm HIGH

104. WESTMORELAND & CUMBERLAND YEOMANRY
QC. ALL SILVER

105

30 mm HIGH

105. ROYAL ANGLIAN REGIMENT
SILVER & GOLD

106

45 mm HIGH

106. THE KING'S OWN ROYAL BORDER REGIMENT
QC. GOLD & SILVER

107

40 mm HIGH

107. ROYAL BERKSHIRE REGIMENT
(Princess Charlotte's of Wales's)
ALL GOLD

108

40 mm HIGH

108. THE BUFFS EAST KENT REGIMENT
ALL GOLD

109

50 mm HIGH

110

40 mm HIGH

111

45 mm HIGH

109. THE BORDER REGIMENT
QC. ALL SILVER WITH HALF RED CENTRE

**110. DUKE OF CORNWALL'S
LIGHT INFANTRY**
ALL SILVER

111. THE CHESHIRE REGIMENT
GOLD & SILVER

112

45 mm HIGH

113

45 mm HIGH

114

30 mm HIGH

112. THE DORSETSHIRE REGIMENT
(Scroll to read Dorsetshire)
GOLD & SILVER

113. THE DORSET REGIMENT
(Scroll to read Dorset)
GOLD & SILVER

**114. THE KING'S OWN ROYAL REGIMENT
(LANCASTER)**
(Lion on a solid tablet)
ALL GOLD

115

40 mm HIGH

116

40 mm HIGH

117

40 mm HIGH

**115. THE NORTHAMPTONSHIRE
REGIMENT**
SILVER & GOLD

116. ROYAL WEST KENT REGIMENT
ALL SILVER

117. ROYAL WARWICKSHIRE REGIMENT
SILVER & GOLD

21

118

43 mm HIGH

118. THE DEVONSHIRE REGIMENT
QC. SILVER & GOLD

119

40 mm HIGH

119. THE ESSEX REGIMENT
GOLD & SILVER

120

47 mm HIGH

120. ROYAL HAMPSHIRE REGIMENT
QC. SILVER & GOLD
QC. ALL BLACK

121

40 mm HIGH

121. PRINCE OF WALES'S VOLUNTEERS
(South Lancashire)
GOLD & SILVER

122

122. PRINCE OF WALES'S VOLUNTEERS
(South Lancashire)
(Beret)

123

30 mm HIGH

123. ROYAL NORFOLK REGIMENT
(Beret)
ALL GOLD

124

124. THE SUFFOLK REGIMENT
QC. SILVER & GOLD

125

40 mm HIGH

125. THE ROYAL SUFFOLK REGIMENT
SILVER & GOLD

126

45 mm HIGH

126. THE LANCASHIRE FUSILIERS
GOLD & SILVER

22

127

50 mm HIGH

127. THE WORCESTERSHIRE REGIMENT
SILVER & GOLD

128

30 mm HIGH

128. ROYAL LEICESTERSHIRE REGIMENT
(Beret)
GOLD & SILVER

129

43 mm HIGH

129. ROYAL NORTHUMBERLAND FUSILIERS
SILVER & GOLD

130

40 mm HIGH

130. THE MIDDLESEX REGIMENT
(Duke of Cambridge's Own)
GOLD & SILVER

131

40 mm HIGH

131. YORK & LANCASTER REGIMENT
GOLD & SILVER

132

42 mm HIGH

132. THE WILTSHIRE REGIMENT
(Duke of Edinburgh's)
ALL GOLD

133

38 mm HIGH

133. THE WILTSHIRE REGIMENT
(Duke of Edinburgh's)
ALL GOLD

134

45 mm HIGH

134. NOTTINGHAMSHIRE & DERBYSHIRE REGIMENT
(Scroll inscribed Notts & Derby) QC. SILVER & GOLD

135

30 mm HIGH

135. THE QUEEN'S ROYAL REGIMENT (WEST SURREY)
(Beret)
ALL GOLD

136

136. THE EAST SURREY REGIMENT
QC. GOLD & SILVER

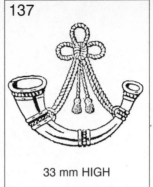

137

33 mm HIGH

**137. OXFORDSHIRE &
BUCKINGHAMSHIRE LIGHT INFANTRY**
(Beret)
ALL SILVER

138

35 mm HIGH

138. THE GREEN HOWARDS
(Alexandra Princess of Wales's Own
Yorkshire Regiment)
ALL SILVER

139

38 mm HIGH

139. THE GREEN HOWARDS
(Alexandra, Princess of Wales's Own
Yorkshire Regiment)
ALL SILVER

140

33 mm HIGH

140. THE DURHAM LIGHT INFANTRY
(Both Beret)
QC. ALL SILVER
QC. ALL BLACK

141

40 mm HIGH

141. WEST YORKSHIRE REGIMENT
(The Prince of Wales's Own)
SILVER & GOLD
ALSO ALL SILVER

142

142. EAST YORKSHIRE REGIMENT
SILVER & GOLD

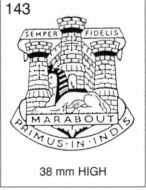

143

38 mm HIGH

143. DEVONSHIRE & DORSET REGIMENT
SILVER & GOLD
ALSO IN ALL BLACK

144

40 mm HIGH

144. THE MANCHESTER REGIMENT
ALL SILVER

145

45 mm HIGH

145. THE LOYAL REGIMENT
(North Lancashire)
(Scroll inscribed The Loyal Regiment)
KC. GOLD & SILVER

146

42 mm HIGH

146. THE LOYAL REGIMENT
(North Lancashire) (Scroll inscribed The Loyal
Regiment) QC. GOLD & SILVER
ALSO FOUND WITH RED ROSE

147

40 mm HIGH

**147. SOUTH STAFFORDSHIRE
REGIMENT**
QC. SILVER & GOLD

148

40 mm HIGH

**148. NORTH STAFFORDSHIRE
REGIMENT**
(The Prince of Wales's)
SILVER & GOLD

149

42 mm HIGH

149. DUKE OF WELLINGTON'S REGIMENT
(West Riding) (There are two versions of this
badge, a one part & a two part badge)
BOTH SILVER & GOLD

150

50 mm HIGH

150. THE RIFLE BRIGADE
(Prince Consort's Own)
KC. ALL SILVER

151

52 mm HIGH

151. THE RIFLE BRIGADE
(Prince Consort's Own)
ALL SILVER

152

152. BEDFORDSHIRE & HERTFORDSHIRE
REGIMENT
ALL SILVER

153

45 mm HIGH

**153. THE EAST LANCASHIRE
REGIMENT**
QC. SILVER & GOLD

154	155	156

42 mm HIGH	20 mm HIGH	
154. THE GLOUCESTERSHIRE REGIMENT ALL SILVER	**155. THE GLOUCESTERSHIRE REGIMENT** (Back Badge) ALL SILVER ALSO IN ALL GOLD	**156. SOMERSET LIGHT INFANTRY** (Prince Albert's) ALL SILVER

157	158	159

38 mm HIGH	38 mm HIGH	50 mm HIGH
157. THE KING'S REGIMENT **(LIVERPOOL)** (Beret) SILVER & GOLD	**158. THE KING'S OWN YORKSHIRE** **LIGHT INFANTRY** ALL SILVER	**159. WORCESTERSHIRE & SHERWOOD** **FORESTERS REGIMENT** (29th/45th Foot) SILVER & GOLD

160	161	162

40 mm HIGH	25 mm HIGH	33 mm HIGH
160. ROYAL LINCOLNSHIRE REGIMENT SILVER & GOLD	**161. DUKE OF EDINBURGH'S ROYAL** **REGIMENT** **(Berkshire & Wiltshire)** SILVER & GOLD	**162. KING'S SHROPSHIRE LIGHT** **INFANTRY** (Both Beret) SILVER & GOLD ALSO IN ALL SILVER

163

43 mm HIGH

163. THE QUEEN'S LANCASHIRE REGIMENT
QC. ALL GOLD WITH RED ROSE
QC. ALL GOLD

164

45 mm HIGH

164. ROYAL GREEN JACKETS
QC. ALL SILVER
QC. ALL BLACK

165

45 mm HIGH

165. THE QUEEN'S REGIMENT
GOLD & SILVER
ALSO ALL BLACK

166

33 mm HIGH

166. THE KING'S REGIMENT
GOLD & SILVER

167

25 mm HIGH

167. THE PRINCE OF WALES'S OWN REGIMENT OF YORKSHIRE
ALL SILVER
ALSO ALL BLACK

168

35 mm HIGH

168. THE STAFFORDSHIRE REGIMENT
(Prince of Wales's)
GOLD & SILVER
ALSO ALL GOLD

169

50 mm HIGH

9. ROYAL REGIMENT OF FUSILIERS
QC. GOLD & SILVER
ALSO ALL BLACK

170

34 mm HIGH

170. THE LIGHT INFANTRY
ALL SILVER

171

50 mm HIGH

171. ROYAL ULSTER RIFLES
KC. ALL SILVER

172

50 mm HIGH

172. ROYAL ULSTER RIFLES
QC. ALL SILVER

173

40 mm HIGH

173. ROYAL IRISH FUSILIERS
(Princess Victoria's)
GOLD & SILVER

174

43 mm HIGH

174. ROYAL INNISKILLING FUSILIER
(Flag flying to the right)
GOLD & SILVER

175

47 mm HIGH

175. ROYAL IRISH RANGERS
((27th Inniskilling) 83rd & 87th)
QC. SILVER & GOLD

176

47 mm HIGH

176. ROYAL IRISH REGIMENT
QC. ALL SILVER

177

40 mm HIGH

177. THE WELCH REGIMENT
SILVER & GOLD

178

40 mm HIGH

178. ROYAL WELCH FUSILIERS
GOLD & SILVER
ALSO ALL GOLD

179

43 mm HIGH

179. SOUTH WALES BORDERERS
GOLD & SILVER
ALSO ALL GOLD

180

43 mm HIGH

180. THE ROYAL REGIMENT OF WAL
(21st/41st Foot)
ALL SILVER
ALSO IN SILVER & GOLD

181

45 mm HIGH

181. THE EAST ANGLIAN BRIGADE
here are two versions of this badge, a one
part & a two part badge)
BOTH SILVER & GOLD

182

34 mm HIGH

182. THE MERCIAN BRIGADE
SILVER & GOLD
ALSO ALL GOLD

183

40 mm HIGH

183. THE HOME COUNTIES BRIGADE
ALL SILVER

184

43 mm HIGH

184. THE FORESTERS BRIGADE
GOLD & SILVER

185

45 mm HIGH

185. THE GREEN JACKETS BRIGADE
QC. ALL SILVER

186

42 mm HIGH

186. THE LANCASTRIAN BRIGADE
QC. GOLD & SILVER

187

34 mm HIGH

7. THE LIGHT INFANTRY BRIGADE
ALL SILVER

188

50 mm HIGH

188. THE FUSILIERS BRIGADE
QC. GOLD & SILVER

189

42 mm HIGH

189. THE NORTH IRISH BRIGADE
QC. SILVER & GOLD

29

190

52 mm HIGH

190. THE LOWLAND BRIGADE
ALL SILVER

191

52 mm HIGH

191. THE HIGHLAND BRIGADE
ALL SILVER

192

38 mm HIGH

192. THE WELSH BRIGADE
ALL SILVER
ALSO ALL GOLD

193

42 mm HIGH

193. THE WESSEX BRIGADE
ALL GOLD
ALSO IN ALL SILVER

194

42 mm HIGH

194. THE YORKSHIRE BRIGADE
(This badge has a space between the bottom of
the rose and the scroll)
QC. SILVER & GOLD

195

42 mm HIGH

195. YORKSHIRE VOLUNTEERS
(This badge is solid between the bottom of
rose and the scroll) QC. SILVER & GOLD
ALSO BLACK & GOLD

196

80 mm HIGH

196. ARGYLL & SUTHERLAND HIGHLANDERS
(Princess Louise's)
ALL SILVER
ALSO ALL BLACK

197

75 mm HIGH

197. THE BLACK WATCH
(Royal Highlanders)
QC. ALL SILVER

198

198. KING'S OWN SCOTTISH BORDERI
QC. ALL SILVER

199 70 mm HIGH

200 43 mm HIGH

201 55 mm HIGH

9. KING'S OWN SCOTTISH BORDERERS
QC. ALL SILVER
ALSO FOUND IN SILVER & GOLD

200. KING'S OWN SCOTTISH BORDERERS
((Size 43mm High (Solid))
QC. ALL SILVER

201. THE CAMERONIANS
(Scottish Rifles)
ALL SILVER

201a 55 mm HIGH

202 68 mm HIGH

203 65 mm HIGH

01a. Q.O. CAMERON HIGHLANDERS
ALL SILVER

202. THE ROYAL HIGHLAND FUSILIERS
(Princess Margaret's Own
Glasgow & Ayrshire Regiment)
QC. GOLD & SILVER

203. THE GORDON HIGHLANDERS
(Bydand spelt as one word)
ALL SILVER

204 65 mm HIGH

205 54 mm HIGH

206 54 mm HIGH

?04. THE GORDON HIGHLANDERS
(By Dand spelt as two words)
ALL SILVER

205. THE HIGHLAND LIGHT INFANTRY
(City of Glasgow Regiment)
KC. ALL SILVER

206. THE HIGHLAND LIGHT INFANTRY
(City of Glasgow Regiment)
QC. ALL SILVER

207

75 mm HIGH

207. ROYAL SCOTS FUSILIERS
KC. ALL GOLD

208

75 mm HIGH

208. ROYAL SCOTS FUSILIERS
QC. ALL GOLD

209

57 mm HIGH

209. THE ROYAL SCOTS
(The Royal Regiment)
SILVER & GOLD

210

55 mm HIGH

210. SEAFORTH HIGHLANDERS
(Ross-Shire Buffs, Duke of Albany's)
ALL SILVER

211

70 mm HIGH

211. QUEEN'S OWN HIGHLANDERS
(Seaforth & Cameron) (Two part badge)
There is a trial version of this badge all in one piece.
BOTH QC. ALL SILVER

212

65 mm HIGH

212. QUEEN'S OWN HIGHLANDERS
(Seaforth & Cameron)
(Pipers)
QC. ALL SILVER

213

213. 1st to 4th CITY OF LONDON REGIMENT
(Royal Fusiliers)
KC. ALL GOLD

214

50 mm HIGH

214. 1st to 4th CITY OF LONDON REGIMENT
(Royal Fusiliers)
QC. ALL GOLD

215

40 mm HIGH

215. 13th LONDON REGIMENT
(Princess Louise's Kensington Regiment)
ALL SILVER

216

50 mm HIGH

216. 14th LONDON REGIMENT
(London Scottish)
ALL SILVER

217

63 mm HIGH

217. 18th LONDON REGIMENT
(London Irish Rifles)
QC. ALL SILVER

218

45 mm HIGH

218. 23rd LONDON REGIMENT
QC. GOLD & SILVER

219

45 mm HIGH

219. COLDSTREAM GUARDS
ALL GOLD

220

45 mm HIGH

220. GRENADIER GUARDS
ALL GOLD

221

45 mm HIGH

221. GRENADIER GUARDS
(N.C.O. & Musicians)
QC. ALL GOLD

222

45 mm HIGH

222. IRISH GUARDS
ALL GOLD

223

45 mm HIGH

223. SCOTS GUARDS
ALL GOLD
ALL BLACK

224

45 mm HIGH

224. SCOTS GUARDS
(Colour Sergeants, Sergeants & Musicians)
SILVER & GOLD

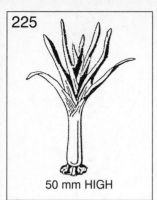

225

50 mm HIGH

225. WELSH GUARDS
ALL GOLD

226

226. GUARDS DEPOT W.R.A.C.
(Scroll inscribed Guards Depot)
QC. ALL GOLD
(Pin Back) (Worn on breast pocket)

227

45 mm HIGH

227. ROYAL ARTILLERY
(There are two versions of this badge, one w
a fixed wheel and one with a moving whee
QC. ALL GOLD

228

40 mm & 35 mm HIGH

228. ROYAL ARTILLERY
(There are two versions of this badge, one with
a fixed wheel and one with a moving wheel)
(Beret) QC. ALL GOLD

229

35 mm HIGH

229. ROYAL HORSE ARTILLERY
(Beret)
QC. ALL SILVER
QC. ALL GOLD

230

230. ARMY CATERING CORPS
KC. GOLD & SILVER

231

38 mm HIGH

231. ARMY CATERING CORPS
QC. GOLD & SILVER

232

40 mm HIGH

232. ARMY CATERING CORPS
QC. GOLD & SILVER

233

45 mm HIGH

233. ROYAL ARMY CHAPLAINS DEP
(Christian)
QC. ALL BLACK

234

234. ROYAL ARMY CHAPLAINS DEPT
(Jewish)
QC. ALL BLACK

235

45 mm HIGH

235. ROYAL ARMY DENTAL CORPS
(There are two versions of this badge, a one part
& a two part badge)
QC. GOLD & SILVER

236

45 mm HIGH

236. ROYAL ARMY EDUCATIONAL
CORPS
QC. GOLD & SILVER

237

237. ROYAL ELECTRICAL & MECHANICAL
ENGINEERS
KC. GOLD & SILVER

238

48 mm HIGH

238. ROYAL ELECTRICAL & MECHANICAL
ENGINEERS
QC. GOLD & SILVER

239

45 mm HIGH

239. ROYAL ENGINEERS
QC. GOLD & SILVER

240

45 mm HIGH

240. ROYAL MONMOUTHSHIRE ROYAL
ENGINEERS (MILITIA)
QC. SILVER & GOLD

241

35 mm HIGH

241. MOBILE DEFENCE CORPS
QC. GOLD & SILVER

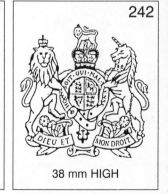

242

38 mm HIGH

242. GENERAL SERVICE CORPS
QC. ALL GOLD

243

38 mm HIGH

243. JUNIOR LEADERS TRAINING REGIMENT
QC. ALL GOLD

244

40 mm HIGH

244. QUEEN ALEXANDRA'S ROYAL ARMY NUSING CORPS
QC. GOLD & SILVER

245

42 mm HIGH

245. ROYAL AIR FORCE
QC. ALL GOLD

246

43 mm HIGH

246. ROYAL ARMY MEDICAL CORPS
(There are two versions of this badge, one with snake in silver and & one with snake in gold.)
QC. GOLD & SILVER

247

42 mm HIGH

247. ROYAL MILITARY POLICE
QC. ALL GOLD

248

248. INTELLIGENCE CORPS
KC. ALL GOLD

249

45 mm HIGH

249. INTELLIGENCE CORPS
QC. ALL GOLD
QC. ALL SILVER

250

40 mm HIGH

250. MILITARY PROVOST STAFF CORPS
QC. ALL GOLD

251

251. ROYAL ARMY ORDNANCE CORP
KC. GOLD & SILVER

252

42 mm HIGH

252. ROYAL ARMY ORDNANCE CORPS
KC. GOLD & SILVER

253

42 mm HIGH

253. ROYAL ARMY ORDNANCE CORPS
QC. GOLD & SILVER
QC. ALL SILVER

254

35 mm HIGH

254. ROYAL PIONEER CORPS
(Beret)
KC. ALL GOLD

255

35 mm HIGH

255. ROYAL PIONEER CORPS
(Beret)
QC. ALL GOLD

256

37 mm HIGH

256. ROYAL PIONEER CORPS
(1980's)
QC. ALL SILVER

257

257. ROYAL ARMY PAY CORPS
(Beret)
KC.

258

43 mm HIGH

258. ROYAL ARMY PAY CORPS
QC. GOLD & SILVER

259

35 mm HIGH

259. ROYAL ARMY PAY CORPS
(Beret)
QC. GOLD & SILVER

260

35 mm HIGH

**260. ARMY PHYSICAL TRAINING
CORPS**
QC. ALL SILVER

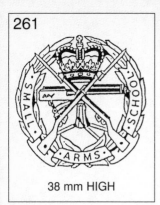

261

38 mm HIGH

261. SMALL ARMS SCHOOL CORPS
QC. ALL SILVER

262

50 mm HIGH

262. ROYAL CORPS OF SIGNALS
(Two Part Badge)
QC. SILVER & GOLD

263

263. ARMY SCRIPTURE READERS
GOLD & SILVER

264

264. ROYAL ARMY SERVICE CORPS
KC. ALL GOLD

265

48 mm HIGH

265. ROYAL ARMY SERVICE CORPS
QC. ALL GOLD

266

48 mm HIGH

266. ROYAL CORPS OF TRANSPORT
QC. SILVER & GOLD

267

43 mm HIGH

267. ROYAL ARMY VETERINARY CORPS
QC. GOLD & SILVER

268

37 mm HIGH

268. WOMEN'S ROYAL ARMY CORPS
QC. GOLD & SILVER
QC. ALL GOLD

269

50 mm HIGH

269. ADJUTANT GENERAL CORPS
QC. GOLD & SILVER

270

45 mm HIGH

270. ADJUTANT GENERAL CORPS
(Size 45mm High)
QC. GOLD & SILVER

271

43 mm HIGH

271. ROYAL LOGISTIC CORPS
QC. GOLD & SILVER

272

40 mm HIGH

272. THE PARACHUTE REGIMENT
KC. ALL SILVER

273

40 mm HIGH

273. THE PARACHUTE REGIMENT
QC. ALL SILVER
QC. ALL BLACK

274

48 mm HIGH

274. ARMY AIR CORPS
QC. ALL SILVER

275

40 mm HIGH

275. SPECIAL AIR SERVICE
GOLD & SILVER

276

276. GLIDER PILOT REGIMENT
KC. ALL SILVER

277

277. GLIDER PILOT REGIMENT
QC. ALL SILVER

278

278. PLYMOUTH DIVISION - THE ROYAL
MARINES (Three Part Badge)
(The plumes on this badge are not anodised,
they are silver metal) KC. GOLD & SILVER

279. PLYMOUTH DIVISION - THE ROYAL MARINES (Three Part Badge)
(The plumes on this badge are not anodised, they are silver metal) QC. GOLD & SILVER

45 mm HIGH

280. THE ROYAL MARINES
QC. ALL GOLD
QC. ALL BLACK

40 mm HIGH

281. ROYAL MARINE CADETS, BAN GOSPORT
ALL GOLD

48 mm HIGH

282. ROYAL MILITARY ACADEMY SANDHURST
QC. ALL SILVER

50 mm HIGH

283. ROYAL HOSPITAL CHELSEA
QC. ALL GOLD

43 mm HIGH

284. ROYAL MILITARY SCHOOL O MUSIC
QC. ALL GOLD

50 mm HIGH

285. ARMY JUNIOR SCHOOL OF MUSIC
QC. ALL SILVER

43 mm HIGH

286. MONS OFFICER CADET SCHOOL
QC. SILVER & GOLD

38 mm HIGH

287. ARMY DEPARTMENT FIRE SERV
(Circlet inscribed Army Fire Service)
QC. ALL SILVER

288

38 mm HIGH

288. ARMY DEPARTMENT FIRE SERVICE
(Circlet inscribed Fire Service W.D)
QC. ALL SILVER

289

289. ROYAL MALTA ARTILLERY
QC. SILVER & GOLD

290

45 mm HIGH

290. ARMY DEPOT POLICE (CYPRUS)
(Scroll inscribed War Dept Police Cyprus)
QC. ALL SILVER

291

45 mm HIGH

291. ARMY DEPOT POLICE (CYPRUS)
(Scroll inscribed Army Depot Police Cyprus)
QC. ALL SILVER

292

50 mm HIGH

292. ARMY APPRENTICES SCHOOL
QC. ALL GOLD
PIPERS IN ALL SILVER

293

45 mm HIGH

293. THE GIBRALTAR REGIMENT
QC. GOLD & SILVER

294

294. WAR DEPT CONSTABULARY
QC. ALL SILVER

295

30 mm HIGH

295. M.O.D. GUARD FORCE
ALL GOLD

296

38 mm HIGH

**296. 2nd KING EDWARD V11's OWN
GURKHA RIFLES**
(The Sirmoor Rifles) (Beret)
ALL BLACK

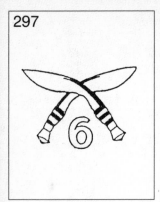

297. 6th QUEEN ELIZABETH'S OWN GURKHA RIFLES
(Beret)
ALL SILVER

30 mm HIGH

298. 6th QUEEN ELIZABETH'S OWN GURKHA RIFLES
(Beret)
QC. ALL SILVER

299. 7th QUEEN ELIZABETH'S OWN GURKHA RIFLES
(Beret)
ALL SILVER

33 mm HIGH

300. DUKE OF EDINBURGH'S OWN GURKHA RIFLES
(There are two versions of this badge, Cypher voided & Cypher non voided) (Beret) ALL SILVER

301. 10th PRINCESS MARY'S OWN GURKHA RIFLES
(There are two versions of this badge, void & non void)
ALL SILVER

25 mm HIGH

302. 10th PRINCESS MARY'S OWN GURKHA RIFLES
(Beret)
ALL SILVER

303. STAFF BAND, THE BRIGADE OF GURKHAS
(Both Beret) ALL SILVER
ALL GOLD

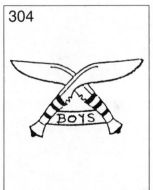

304. BOYS COMPANY, THE BRIGADE OF GURKHAS
(Beret)
ALL SILVER

30 mm HIGH

305. THE QUEEN'S GURKHA ENGINEERS
(Beret) ALL SILVER
ALSO SILVER & GOLD

306

38 mm HIGH

306. THE QUEEN'S GURKHA SIGNALS
(Two Part Badge)
QC. SILVER & GOLD

307

43 mm HIGH

307. GURKHA TRANSPORT REGIMENT
(Scroll inscribed Gurkha Transport Regiment)
QC. GOLD & SILVER

308

308. GURKHA ARMY SERVICE CORPS
(Scroll inscribed Gurkha Army Service Corps)
QC. GOLD & SILVER

309

45 mm HIGH

309. GURKHA MILITARY POLICE
QC. ALL GOLD
QC. ALL SILVER

310

310. ROYAL BERKSHIRE TERRITORIALS
ALL SILVER

311

42 mm HIGH

311. THE BEDFORDSHIRE REGIMENT
ALL SILVER

312

40 mm HIGH

**312. BEDFORDSHIRE & HERTFORD-
SHIRE REGIMENT**
GOLD & SILVER

313

48 mm HIGH

313. THE BUCKINGHAMSHIRE BATTALION
QC. ALL BLACK

314

47 mm HIGH

314. DEVONSHIRE TERRITORIALS
QC. GOLD & SILVER

315

40 mm HIGH

315. THE DORSET TERRITORIALS
ALL SILVER

316

45 mm HIGH

316. HAMPSHIRE & ISLE OF WIGHT TERRITORIALS
QC. GOLD & SILVER

317

40 mm HIGH

317. HEREFORSHIRE LIGHT INFANTRY
ALL SILVER

318

45 mm HIGH

318. THE QUEEN'S ROYAL SURREY REGIMENT
QC. GOLD & SILVER

319

45 mm HIGH

319. HONOURABLE ARTILLERY COMPANY
QC. ALL GOLD

320

35 mm HIGH

320. HONOURABLE ARTILLERY COMPANY
(Beret)
QC. ALL GOLD

321

55 mm HIGH

321. HONOURABLE ARTILLERY COMPANY
ALL SILVER
ALSO IN SILVER & GOLD

322

50 mm HIGH

322. THE ROBIN HOOD BATTALION
(Nottinghamshire & Derbyshire Regiment)
QC. ALL SILVER

323

42 mm HIGH

323. THE KING'S REGIMENT (LIVERPOOL)
8th (Irish) Battalion
Scroll inscribed 8th (Irish) Bn
The King's Regiment L'pool   QC. ALL SILVER

324

35 mm HIGH

324. THE ROYAL HAMPSHIRE REGIMENT
(Duke of Connaught's 6th Royal Hampshire R.A.)
ALL SILVER

325

40 mm HIGH

325. SUFFOLK & CAMBRIDGESHIRE REGIMENT
QC. SILVER & GOLD

326

50 mm HIGH

326. THE OXFORDSHIRE TERRITORIALS
ALL SILVER

327

35 mm HIGH

327. ROYAL WILTSHIRE TERRITORIALS
QC. GOLD & SILVER

328

42 mm HIGH

328. THE WESSEX REGIMENT
ALL GOLD

329

329. THE STAFFORDSHIRE REGIMENT
(The Prince of Wales's)
5th/6th (Territorial) Bn
ALL GOLD

330

45 mm HIGH

330. LONDON YEOMANRY & TERRITORIALS
QC. ALL SILVER

331

70 mm HIGH

331. THE HIGHLAND LIGHT INFANTRY
(City of Glasgow Regiment)
The Glasgow Highlanders
QC. ALL SILVER

332

55 mm HIGH

332. QUEEN'S OWN CAMERON HIGHLANDERS
(Liverpool Scottish)
ALL SILVER

332a

55 mm HIGH

332a. 5th Bn SEAFORTH HIGHLANDERS
ALL SILVER

333

50 mm HIGH

333. P.W.O. REGIMENT OF YORKSHIRE
(The Leeds Rifles) (Scroll inscribed 7th Bn
PWO The West Yorkshire Regiment)
QC. ALL SILVER

334

50 mm HIGH

334. P.W.O. REGIMENT OF YORKSHIRE
(The Leeds Rifles)
(Scroll inscribed The Leeds Rifles)
QC. ALL SILVER

335

40 mm HIGH

335. ULSTER DEFENCE REGIMENT
QC. ALL GOLD
QC. ALL BLACK

336

50 mm HIGH

336. GLOUCESTERSHIRE & HAMPSHIRE
QC. SILVER & GOLD

337

47 mm HIGH

337. ROYAL ALDERNEY MILITIA
QC. ALL GOLD

338

45 mm HIGH

338. ROYAL JERSEY MILITIA R.E.
QC. SILVER & GOLD

339

No illustration available

339. ROYAL GUERNSEY MILITIA

340

50 mm HIGH

340. ABERDEEN UNIVERSITY
ALL SILVER

341

53 mm HIGH

341. BELFAST (QUEEN'S UNIVERSITY O.T.C)
QC. ALL GOLD   QC. ALL SILVER FOR PIPERS
(Also one collar size worn by officers)
ALL GOLD

342

40 mm HIGH

342. BIRMINGHAM UNIVERSITY O.T.C.
ALL GOLD

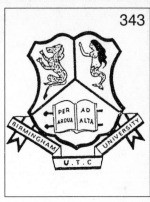

343

343. BIRMINGHAM UNIVERSITY U.T.C.

344

344. BIRMINGHAM UNIVERSITY O.T.C.
ALL SILVER

345

35 mm HIGH

345. BRISTOL UNIVERSITY O.T.C.
(There are two versions of this badge to be found
with slightly different design to horse)
BOTH ALL GOLD

346

45 mm HIGH

346. CAMBRIDGE UNIVERSITY O.T.C.
QC. ALL SILVER

347

347. CARDIFF UNIVERSITY O.T.C.

348

33 mm HIGH

348. DURHAM UNIVERSITY O.T.C.
(Now Northumberian Universities O.T.C.)
ALL GOLD
ALSO ALL SILVER

349

50 mm HIGH

349. EDINBURGH UNIVERSITY O.T.C.
(Now Edinburgh & Herriot-Watt Universities O.T.C.)
QC. SILVER & GOLD

47

350

58 mm HIGH

350. EDINBURGH UNIVERSITY O.T.C.
(Now Edinburgh & Herriot-Watt
Universities O.T.C.)
QC. ALL SILVER

351

38 mm HIGH

351. LIVERPOOL UNIVERSITY O.T.C.
SILVER & GOLD

352

352. UNIVERSITY OF LONDON O.T.C.
KC. ALL GOLD

353

43 mm HIGH

353. UNIVERSITY OF LONDON O.T.C.
QC. ALL GOLD
QC. ALL SILVER

354

45 mm HIGH

354. LEEDS UNIVERSITY O.T.C.
(Scroll inscribed Officers Training Corps)
ALL GOLD

355

38 mm HIGH

355. MANCHESTER UNIVERSITY O.T.C.
(Now Manchester & Salford Universities O.T.C.)
ALL GOLD

356

45 mm HIGH

356. NOTTINGHAM UNIVERSITY O.T.C.
(Now East Midlands Universities O.T.C.)
(Scroll inscribed Nottingham)
QC. SILVER & GOLD

357

45 mm HIGH

357. NOTTINGHAM UNIVERSITY O.T.C.
(Now East Midlands Universities O.T.C.)
(Scroll inscribed East Midlands)
QC. SILVER & GOLD

358

48 mm HIGH

358. OXFORD UNIVERSITY O.T.C.
QC. ALL SILVER
ALSO FOUND WITH KC.
ALSO ALL SILVER

359. ST. ANDREW'S UNIVERSITY O.T.C.
(Now Tayforth Universities O.T.C.)
(Scroll inscribed St. Andrew's University O.T.C.)
KC.

43 mm HIGH

360. ST. ANDREW'S UNIVERSITY U.T.C.
(Now Tayforth Universities U.T.C.)
(Scroll inscribed St. Andrew's University U.T.C.)
KC. ALL GOLD

361. SHEFFIELD UNIVERSITY O.T.C.
(Scroll inscribed Sheffield University O.T.C.)

362. SHEFFIELD UNIVERSITY U.T.C.
(Scroll inscribed Sheffield University U.T.C.)

45 mm HIGH

363. SHEFFIELD UNIVERSITY O.T.C.
(Scroll inscribed University of Sheffield O.T.C.)
ALL GOLD

47 mm HIGH

364. SOUTHAMPTON UNIVERSITY O.T.C.
ALL GOLD

75 mm HIGH

365. TAYFORTH UNIVERSITIES O.T.C.
(St. Andrew's, Dundee, Stirling)
(Scroll inscribed Tayforth U.O.T.C.)
ALL SILVER ALSO IN SILVER & GOLD

50 mm HIGH

366. GLASGOW UNIVERSITY O.T.C.
(Now Glasgow & Strathclyde Universities O.T.C.)
(Scroll inscribed Glasgow & Strathclyde U.O.T.C.)
ALL GOLD

367. UNIVERSITY OF WALES O.T.C.
ALL GOLD

49

368. BLOXHAM SCHOOL, OXON

369. BANCROFT'S SCHOOL C.C.F.

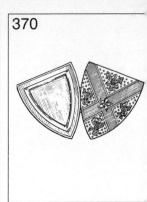

370. BARNARD CASTLE SCHOOL C.C.F.

33 mm HIGH

371. CHRIST'S HOSPITAL, HORSHAM
(Worn by C.C.F.)
ALL GOLD

40 mm HIGH

**372. DUKE OF YORK'S ROYAL
MILITARY SCHOOL DOVER**
QC. GOLD & SILVER

30 mm HIGH

373. ESPOM COLLEGE C.C.F.
ALL GOLD

374. EXETER SCHOOL C.C.F.
(Circlet inscribed Exeter School C.C.F.)
KC. ALL GOLD

40 mm HIGH

375. EXETER UNIVERSITY O.T.C.
GOLD & SILVER

**376. GORDON BOYS SCHOOL OLD
WOKING, SURREY**
ALL GOLD

377

377. K.E.S BIRMINGHAM C.C.F.
ALL SILVER

378

378. ARDINGLEY C.C.F.

379

43 mm HIGH

379. KING'S SCHOOL, ROCHESTER
(Scroll inscribed King's School Rochester C.C.F.)
ALL GOLD

380

58 mm HIGH

380. LIVERPOOL COLLEGE C.C.F.
(Circlet inscribed Liverpool College C.C.F.)
ALL GOLD

381

381. MERCERS SCHOOL

382

382. MERCHANT TAYLORS SCHOOL
ALL GOLD

383

38 mm HIGH

383. MILLFIELD SCHOOL C.C.F.
ALL SILVER

384

384. MILL HILL SCHOOL O.T.C.

385

385. MONMOUTH SCHOOL
ALL GOLD

386. OAKHAM SCHOOL O.T.C.

387. OUNDLE SCHOOL

**388. QUEEN VICTORIA SCHOOL
DUNBLANE**
QC. ALL SILVER

38 mm HIGH

389. REPTON SCHOOL, DERBY
(Scroll inscribed Repton C.C.F.)
ALL GOLD

43 mm HIGH

390. ST. DUNSTANS COLLEGE C.C.F.
(Top scroll inscribed St. Dunstan's College)
(Bottom scroll inscribed Albam C.C.F Exorna)
ALL GOLD

391. ST. LAWRENCE COLLEGE O.T.C.

45 mm HIGH

392. STOWE SCHOOL BUCKS
(WORN BY C.C.F.)
ALL SILVER

43 mm HIGH

393. TONBRIDGE SCHOOL KENT
(Scroll inscribed Tonbridge School O.T.C.)
ALL GOLD
ALSO ALL SILVER

394. CLIFTON COLLEGE C.C.F.
ALL GOLD

52

395

396

397

5. HURSTPIERPOINT COLLEGE C.C.F.
ALL GOLD

396. MARLBOROUGH COLLEGE
ALL GOLD

397. PERSE SCHOOL C.C.F.

398

399

38 mm HIGH

400

40 mm HIGH

398. ST. EDMUNDS SCHOOL C.C.F
(Scroll inscribed St. Edmunds School C.C.F.)
ALL GOLD

399. WELBECK COLLEGE, WORKSOP NOTTS
GOLD & SILVER

400. WELLINGTON COLLEGE, BERKS
ALL GOLD
ALSO ALL SILVER

401

402

403

33 mm HIGH

01. WELLINGTON SCHOOL, SOMERSET
ALL GOLD

402. WINCHESTER COLLEGE

403. UNIVERSITY O.T.C. CARDIFF
ALL GOLD

45 mm HIGH

404. UNIVERSITY OF WALES O.T.C
ALL GOLD

405. SOLIHULL SCHOOL C.C.F.
(Scroll inscribed Solihull School C.C.F.)
ALL SILVER

406. LEEDS UNIVERSITY O.T.C.
(Circlet inscribed Training Corps and Scroll
inscribed Leeds University)
ALL GOLD

INDEX

55 THE SHROPSHIRE YEOMANRY
Sealed 14th November 1950
56 THE SHROPSHIRE YEOMANRY
Sealed 8th April 1957
57 QUEEN'S OWN MERCIAN YEOMANRY
58 THE SHERWOOD RANGERS YEOMANRY
59 THE SHERWOOD RANGERS YEOMANRY
60 THE SHERWOOD RANGERS YEOMANRY
61 THE SUSSEX YEOMANRY
Sealed 5th May 1952
62 THE SUSSEX YEOMANRY
Sealed 8th January 1957
63 LEICESTERSHIRE & DERBYSHIRE
YEOMANRY
Sealed 14th March 1957
64 THE NORFOLK YEOMANRY
Sealed 17th October 1953
65 LOYAL SUFFOLK HUSSARS
66 LOYAL SUFFOLK HUSSARS
Sealed 14th September 1953
67 SUFFOLK & NORFOLK YEOMANRY
68 THE STAFFORDSHIRE YEOMANRY
Sealed 8th August 1952
69 THE STAFFORDSHIRE YEOMANRY
70 QUEEN'S OWN WORCESTERSHIRE
HUSSARS
Sealed 16th November 1951
71 THE QUEEN'S OWN YORKSHIRE
DRAGOONS
72 QUEEN'S OWN OXFORDSHIRE HUSSARS
Sealed 9th May 1952
73 QUEEN'S OWN ROYAL GLASGOW
YEOMANRY
74 THE SCOTTISH HORSE
Sealed 30th October 1951
75 THE LOTHIANS & BORDER HORSE
Sealed 11th January 1962
76 THE WARWICKSHIRE YEOMANRY
77 QUEEN'S OWN WARWICKSHIRE &
WORCESTERSHIRE YEOMANRY
78 ROYAL GLOUCESTERSHIRE HUSSARS
79 NORTH IRISH HORSE
80 THE CITY OF LONDON YEOMANRY
Sealed 3rd April 1959
81 THE KENT & COUNTY OF LONDON
YEOMANRY

82 DENBIGHSHIRE YEOMANRY
Sealed 28th January 1952
83 DENBIGHSHIRE YEOMANRY
Sealed 28th January 1958
84 ROYAL WILTSHIRE YEOMANRY
85 PEMBROKE YEOMANRY
86 PEMBROKE YEOMANRY
87 SOUTH NOTTINGHAMSHIRE HUSSARS
Sealed 14th February 1952
88 THE INNS OF COURT REGIMENT
Sealed 13th November 1958
89 INNS OF COURT & CITY YEOMANRY
90 1st COUNTY OF LONDON YEOMANRY
91 HERTFORDSHIRE YEOMANRY
Sealed 21st May 1955
92 HERTFORDSHIRE & BEDFORDSHIRE
YEOMANRY
93 THE HIGHLAND YEOMANRY
Sealed 7th April 1960
94 QUEEN'S OWN LOWLAND YEOMANRY
95 QUEEN'S OWN DORSET & WEST
SOMERSET YEOMANRY
96 THE LEICESTERSHIRE YEOMANRY
97 THE DUKE OF LANCASTER'S OWN
YEOMANRY
Sealed 17th September 1951
98 THE EAST RIDING YEOMANRY
Sealed 11th March 1952
99 HAMPSHIRE CARABINIERS YEOMANRY
100 THE FIFE & FORFAR YEOMANRY
101 QUEEN'S OWN YEOMANRY
Sealed 29th March 1972
102 NORTH SOMERSET & BRISTOL
YEOMANRY
103 THE LOVAT SCOUTS
Sealed 10th January 1951
104 WESTMORELAND & CUMBERLAND
YEOMANRY

INFANTRY
105 ROYAL ANGLIAN REGIMENT
Sealed 25th March 1954
106 THE KING'S OWN ROYAL BORDER
REGIMENT
107 ROYAL BERKSHIRE REGIMENT

108 THE BUFFS (EAST KENT REGIMENT)
Sealed 14th January 1964
109 THE BORDER REGIMENT
110 CORNWALL LIGHT INFANTRY
Sealed 4th February 1964
111 THE CHESHIRE REGIMENT
Sealed 26th May 1966
112 THE DORSETSHIRE REGIMENT
113 THE DORSETSHIRE REGIMENT
Sealed 4th October 1956
114 THE KING'S OWN ROYAL REGIMENT
(LANCASTER)
Sealed 17th October 1954
115 THE NORTHAMPTONSHIRE REGIMENT
Sealed 6th May 1965
116 THE ROYAL WEST KENT REGIMENT
Sealed 2nd November 1964
117 ROYAL WARWICKSHIRE REGIMENT
118 THE DEVONSHIRE REGIMENT
119 THE ESSEX REGIMENT
Sealed 1st February 1966
120 ROYAL HAMPSHIRE REGIMENT
Sealed 12th May 1971
121 P.W.V. SOUTH LANCASHIRE REGIMENT
Sealed 17th October 1963
122 P.W.V. SOUTH LANCASHIRE REGIMENT
Sealed 22nd February 1965
123 ROYAL NORFOLK REGIMENT
Sealed 21st April 1964
124 THE SUFFOLK REGIMENT
125 THE ROYAL SUSSEX REGIMENT
Sealed 4th May 1954
126 THE LANCASHIRE FUSILIERS
127 THE WORCESTERSHIRE REGIMENT
128 ROYAL LEICESTERSHIRE REGIMENT
Sealed 11th July 1968
129 THE ROYAL NORTHUMBERLAND
FUSILIERS
130 THE MIDDLESEX REGIMENT
Sealed 22nd June 1964
131 YORK & LANCASTER REGIMENT
Sealed 1st November 1963
132 THE WILTSHIRE REGIMENT
133 THE WILTSHIRE REGIMENT
Sealed 26th August 1964
134 NOTTS & DERBY REGIMENT

135 THE QUEEN'S ROYAL REGIMENT (WEST
SURREY)
Sealed 18th August 1961
136 THE EAST SURREY REGIMENT
137 OXFORDSHIRE & BUCKINGHAMSHIRE
LIGHT INFANTRY
Sealed 28th August 1964
138 THE GREEN HOWARDS
139 THE GREEN HOWARDS
140 THE DURHAM LIGHT INFANTRY
141 WEST YORKSHIRE REGIMENT
142 EAST YORKSHIRE REGIMENT
Sealed 20th March 1955
143 DEVON & DORSET REGIMENT
144 THE MANCHESTER REGIMENT
Sealed 24th August 196
145 THE LOYAL REGIMENT
146 THE LOYAL REGIMENT
147 SOUTH STAFFORDSHIRE REGIMENT
Sealed 21st January 1966
148 NORTH STAFFORDSHIRE REGIMENT
Sealed 28th April 1966
149 DUKE OF WELLINGTON'S REGIMENT
(WEST RIDING)
Sealed 7th April 1970
150 THE RIFLE BRIGADE
151 THE RIFLE BRIGADE
152 BEDFORDSHIRE & HERTFORDSHIRE
REGIMENT
153 THE EAST LANCASHIRE REGIMENT
Sealed 26th May 1966
154 THE GLOUCESTERSHIRE REGIMENT
155 THE GLOUCESTERSHIRE REGIMENT
(BACK BADGE)
Sealed 20th March 1967
156 SOMERSET LIGHT INFANTRY
157 THE KING'S REGIMENT   (LIVERPOOL)
Sealed 22th November 1971
158 KING'S OWN YORKSHIRE LIGHT
INFANTRY
Sealed 25th April 1951
159 WORCESTERSHIRE & SHERWOOD
FORESTERS REGIMENT
160 ROYAL LINCOLNSHIRE REGIMENT
Sealed 11th March 1965
161 BERKSHIRE & WILTSHIRE REGIMENT

162 KING'S SHROPSHIRE LIGHT INFANTRY
   Sealed 14th August 1963
163 THE QUEEN'S LANCASHIRE REGIMENT
164 ROYAL GREEN JACKETS
165 THE QUEEN'S REGIMENT
   Sealed 10th July 1966
166 THE KING'S REGIMENT
   Sealed 22nd November 1971
167 THE PRINCE OF WALES'S OWN
REGIMENT OF YORKSHIRE
168 THE STAFFORDSHIRE REGIMENT
169 THE ROYAL REGIMENT OF FUSILIERS
170 THE LIGHT INFANTRY
171 ROYAL ULSTER RIFLES
172 ROYAL ULSTER RIFLES
   Sealed 28th May 1964
173 ROYAL IRISH FUSILIERS
174 ROYAL INNISKILLING FUSILIERS
175 ROYAL IRISH RANGERS
176 ROYAL IRISH REGIMENT
   Sealed 11th June 1993
177 THE WELCH REGIMENT
   Sealed 24th August 1964
178 ROYAL WELCH FUSILIERS
   Sealed 27th April 1962
179 SOUTH WALES BORDERERS
   Sealed 8th April 1964
180 ROYAL REGIMENT OF WALES
181 THE EAST ANGLIAN BRIGADE
   Sealed 28th May 1958
182 THE MERCIAN BRIGADE
183 THE HOME COUNTIES BRIGADE
   Sealed 22nd May 1958
184 THE FORESTER BRIGADE
   Sealed 14th April 1959
185 THE GREEN JACKETS BRIGADE
   Sealed 7th October 1958
186 THE LANCASTRIAN BRIGADE
187 THE LIGHT INFANTRY BRIGADE
188 THE FUSILIER BRIGADE
   Sealed 5th September 1958
189 THE NORTH IRISH BRIGADE
   Sealed 8th December 1958
190 THE LOWLAND BRIGADE
   Sealed 17th November 1958
191 THE HIGHLAND BRIGADE

192 THE WELSH BRIGADE
193 THE WESSEX BRIGADE
194 THE YORKSHIRE BRIGADE
195 THE YORKSHIRE VOLUNTEERS
196 ARGYLL & SUTHERLAND HIGHLANDERS
197 THE BLACK WATCH
198 KING'S OWN SCOTTISH BORDERERS
199 KING'S OWN SCOTTISH BORDERERS
200 KING'S OWN SCOTTISH BORDERERS
201 THE CAMERONIANS
201a QUEEN'S OWN CAMERON
   HIGHLANDERS
   Sealed 8th January 1965
202 THE ROYAL HIGHLAND FUSILIERS
203 THE GORDON HIGHLANDERS
204 THE GORDON HIGHLANDERS
205 THE HIGHLAND LIGHT INFANTRY
206 THE HIGHLAND LIGHT INFANTRY
207 ROYAL SCOTS FUSILIERS
208 ROYAL SCOTS FUSILIERS
   Sealed 11th July 1957
209 THE ROYAL SCOTS
210 SEAFORTH HIGHLANDERS
   Sealed 6th November 1964
211 SEAFORTH & CAMERONS
212 SEAFORTH & CAMERONS (PIPERS)

LONDON REGIMENTS
213 ROYAL FUSILIERS
214 ROYAL FUSILIERS
215 13th LONDON REGIMENT
   13th March 1963
216 14th LONDON REGIMENT
   Sealed 27th June 1964
217 18th LONDON REGIMENT
   Sealed 5th March 1957
218 23rd LONDON REGIMENT
   Sealed 28th January 1958

GUARDS
219 COLDSTREAM GUARDS
   Sealed 20th May 1958
220 GRENADIER GUARDS
   Sealed 19th March 1962
221 GRENADIER GUARDS
   Sealed 20th September 1963

222 IRISH GUARDS
   Sealed 20th May 1953
223 SCOTS GUARDS
   Sealed 20th May 1958
224 SCOTS GUARDS
   Sealed 20th June 1964
225 WELSH GUARDS
226 GUARDS DEPOT W.R.A.C.

DEPARTMENT & CORPS
227 ROYAL ARTILLERY
   Sealed 23rd June 1954
228 ROYAL ARTILLERY
229 ROYAL HORSE ARTILLERY
   Sealed 22nd March 1966
230 ARMY CATERING CORPS
231 ARMY CATERING CORPS
232 ARMY CATERING CORPS
233 ROYAL ARMY CHAPLAINS DEPT
   (CHRISTIAN)
234 ROYAL ARMY CHAPLAINS DEPT (JEWISH)
235 ROYAL ARMY DENTAL CORPS
236 ROYAL ARMY EDUCATIONAL CORPS
237 ROYAL ELECTRICAL & MECHANICAL
   ENGINEERS
238 ROYAL ELECTRICAL & MECHANICAL
   ENGINEERS
   Sealed 25th September 1963
239 ROYAL ENGINEERS
240 ROYAL MONMOUTHSHIRE R.E. MILITIA
241 MOBILE DEFENCE FORCE
242 GENERAL SERVICE CORPS
243 JUNIOR LEADERS TRAINING REGIMENT
244 QUEEN ALEXANDRA'S ROYAL ARMY
   NURSING CORPS
245 ROYAL AIR FORCE
246 ROYAL ARMY MEDICAL CORPS
247 ROYAL MILITARY POLICE
248 INTELLIGENCE CORPS
249 INTELLIGENCE CORPS
250 MILITARY PROVOST STAFF CORPS
251 ROYAL ARMY ORDNANCE CORPS
252 ROYAL ARMY ORDNANCE CORPS
253 ROYAL ARMY ORDNANCE CORPS
254 ROYAL PIONEER CORPS
255 ROYAL PIONEER CORPS

256 ROYAL PIONEER CORPS
   Sealed 25th February 1985
257 ROYAL ARMY PAY CORPS
258 ROYAL ARMY PAY CORPS
259 ROYAL ARMY PAY CORPS
260 ARMY PHYSICAL TRAINING CORPS
261 SMALL ARMS SCHOOL CORPS
   Sealed 6th September 1956
262 ROYAL CORPS OF SIGNALS
   Sealed 31st March 1955
263 ARMY SCRIPTURE READERS
264 ROYAL ARMY SERVICE CORPS
265 ROYAL ARMY SERVICE CORPS
   Sealed 16th August 196
266 ROYAL CORPS OF TRANSPORT
267 ROYAL ARMY VETERINARY CORPS
268 WOMEN'S ROYAL ARMY CORPS

269 ADJUTANT GENERAL CORPS
   Sealed 5th June 1992
270 ADJUTANT GENERAL CORPS
   Sealed 6th February 1994
271 ROYAL LOGISTIC CORPS

AIRBORNE FORCES
272 THE PARACHUTE REGIMENT
273 THE PARACHUTE REGIMENT
   Sealed 18th April 1966
274 ARMY AIR CORPS
275 SPECIAL AIR SERVICE
276 THE GLIDER PILOT REGIMENT
   Sealed 10th November 1950
277 THE GLIDER PILOT REGIMENT
   Sealed 12th October 1955

ROYAL MARINES
278 ROYAL MARINES (PLYMOUTH DIVISION)
279 ROYAL MARINES (PLYMOUTH DIVISION)
280 ROYAL MARINES
281 ROYAL MARINE CADETS, BAND GOSPORT

SCHOOLS & MISCELLANEOUS
282 ROYAL MILITARY ACADEMY
   SANDHURST

283 ROYAL HOSPITAL CHELSEA
  Sealed 4rd August 1954
284 ROYAL MILITARY SCHOOL OF MUSIC
285 ARMY JUNIOR SCHOOL OF MUSIC
286 MONS OFFICER CADET SCHOOL
287 ARMY DEPARTMENT FIRE SERVICE
288 ARMY DEPARTMENT FIRE SERVICE
289 ROYAL MALTA ARTILLERY
290 ARMY DEPOT POLICE (CYPRUS)
291 ARMY DEPOT POLICE (CYPRUS)
292 ARMY APPRENTICES SCHOOL
293 THE GIBRALTAR REGIMENT
294 WAR DEPARTMENT REGIMENT
295 M.O.D. GUARD FORCE

BRIGADE OF GURKHAS
296 2nd GURKHA RIFLES
297 6th GURKHA RIFLES
298 6th GURKHA RIFLES
299 7th GURKHA RIFLES
300 7th GURKHA RIFLES
301 10th GURKHA RIFLES
302 10th GURKHA RIFLES
  Sealed 30th June 1961
303 STAFF BAND BRIGADE OF GURKHAS
304 BOYS COMPANY, THE BRIGADE OF
  GURKHAS
305 THE QUEEN'S GURKHA ENGINEERS
  Sealed 19th November 1958
306 THE QUEEN'S GURKHA SIGNALS
307 GURKHA TRANSPORT REGIMENT
308 GURKHA ARMY SERVICE CORPS
309 GURKHA MILITARY POLICE
  Sealed 23rd June 1959
309a ROYAL GURKHA RIFLES

TERRITORIAL REGIMENTS
310 ROYAL BERKSHIRE TERRITORIALS
311 THE BEDFORDSHIRE REGIMENT
  Sealed 1st January 1960
312 BEDFORDSHIRE & HERTFORDSHIRE
  REGIMENT
313 THE BUCKINGHAMSHIRE BATTALION
314 DEVONSHIRE TERRITORIALS
315 THE DORSET TERRITORIALS

316 HAMPSHIRE & ISLE OF WIGHT
TERRITORIALS
317 HERTFORDSHIRE LIGHT INFANTRY
318 ROYAL SURREY REGIMENT
319 HONOURABLE ARTILLERY COMPANY
  (ARTILLERY)
320 HONOURABLE ARTILLERY COMPANY
  (ARTILLERY)
321 HONOURABLE ARTILLERY COMPANY
  (INFANTRY)
322 ROBIN HOODS (TERRITORIAL) Bn
323 THE KING'S REGIMENT (LIVERPOOL) 8th
  (IRISH) Bn
324 6th ROYAL HAMPSHIRE R.A.
325 SUFFOLK & CAMBRIDGESHIRE
  REGIMENT
326 THE OXFORDSHIRE TERRITORIALS
327 ROYAL WILTSHIRE TERRITORIALS
328 THE WESSEX REGIMENT
329 THE STAFFORDSHIRE REGIMENT 5th /6th
  (TERRITORIAL) Bn
330 LONDON YEOMANRY & TERRITORIALS
331 THE GLASGOW HIGHLANDERS
  Sealed 19th February 1957
332 CAMERON HIGHLANDERS (LIVERPOOL
  SCOTTISH)
333 7th Bn P.W.O. THE WEST YORKSHIRE
  REGIMENT
334 THE LEEDS RIFLES
335 ULSTER DEFENCE REGIMENT
336 GLOUCESTERSHIRE & HAMPSHIRE
  REGIMENT
337 ROYAL ALDERNEY MILITIA
338 ROYAL JERSEY MILITIA R.E.
339 ROYAL GUERNESY MILITIA (Not illustrated)
  O.T.C. (SENIOR DIVISION)
340 ABERDEEN UNIVERSITY O.T.C.
341 BELFAST (QUEEN'S UNIVERSITY O.T.C.)
342 BIRMINGHAM UNIVERSITY O.T.C.
  Sealed 24th. August 1950
343 BIRMINGHAM UNIVERSITY U.T.C.
344 BIRMINGHAM UNIVERSITY O.T.C.
345 BRISTOL UNIVERSITY O.T.C.
346 CAMBRIDGE UNIVERSITY O.T.C.
347 CARDIFF UNIVERSITY O.T.C.
348 DURHAM UNIVERSITY O.T.C.

349 EDINBURGH UNIVERSITY O.T.C.
350 EDINBURGH UNIVERSITY O.T.C.
351 LIVERPOOL UNIVERSITY O.T.C.
352 UNIVERSITY OF LONDON O.T.C.
353 UNIVERSITY OF LONDON O.T.C.
354 LEEDS UNIVERSITY O.T.C.
355 MANCHESTER UNIVERSITY O.T.C.
   Sealed 18th July 1950
356 NOTTINGHAM UNIVERSITY O.T.C.
   (NOTTINGHAM)
357 NOTTINGHAM UNIVERSITY O.T.C. (EAST
   MIDLANDS)
358 OXFORD UNIVERSITY O.T.C.
359 ST .ANDREWS UNIVERSITY O.T.C.
360 ST. ANDREWS UNIVERSITY U.T.C.
   Sealed 26th January 1951
361 SHEFFIELD UNIVERSITY O.T.C.
362 SHEFFIELD UNIVERSITY U.T.C.
363 UNIVERSITY OF SHEFFIELD O.T.C.
364 SOUTHAMPTON UNIVERSITY O.T.C.
365 TAYFORTH UNIVERSITY O.T.C.
366 GLASGOW UNIVERSITY O.T.C.
367 UNIVERSITY OF WALES O.T.C.
   Sealed 24th August 1950
   O.T.C. (JUNIOR DIVISION)
368 BLOXHAM SCHOOL, OXON
369 BANCROFT SCHOOL C.C.F.
370 BARNARD CASTLE SCHOOL C.C.F.
371 CHRIST'S HOSPITAL, HORSHAM
372 DUKE OF YORK'S ROYAL MILITARY
   SCHOOL, DOVER
373 EPSOM COLLEGE C.C.F.
374 EXETER SCHOOL C.C.F.
375 EXETER UNIVERSITY O.T.C.

376 GORDON BOYS SCHOOL OLD WOKING,
   SURREY
377 K.E.S. BIRMINGHAM C.C.F.
378 ARDINGLEY C.C.F.
379 KING'S SCHOOL ROCHESTER
380 LIVERPOOL COLLEGE C.C.F.
381 MERCERS SCHOOL
382 MERCHANT TAYLORS SCHOOL
383 MILLFIELD SCHOOL C.C.F.
384 MILL HILL SCHOOL O.T.C.
385 MONMOUTH SCHOOL
386 OAKHAM SCHOOL O.T.C.
387 OUNDLE SCHOOL
388 QUEEN VICTORIA SCHOOL, DUNBLANE
   Sealed 7th December 1964
389 REPTON SCHOOL C.C.F.
390 ST. DUNSTANS COLLEGE C.C.F.
391 ST. LAWRENCE COLLEGE O.T.C.
392 STOWE SCHOOL, BUCKS
393 TONBRIDGE SCHOOL, KENT
394 CLIFTON COLLEGE C.C.F.
395 HURSTPIERPOINT COLLEGE C.C.F.
396 MARLBOROUGH COLLEGE
397 PERSE SCHOOL C.C.F.
398 ST. EDMUNDS SCHOOL O.T.C.
399 WELBECK COLLEGE, WORKSOP, NOTTS
400 WELLINGTON COLLEGE, BERKS
401 WELLINGTON SCHOOL, SOMERSET
402 WINCHESTER COLLEGE
403 UNIVERSITY O.T.C. CARDIFF
404 UNIVERSITY OF WALES O.T.C.
405 SOLIHULL SCHOOL C.C.F.
406 LEEDS UNIVERSITY O.T.C.

Patterns Sealed

THE LIFE GUARDS
Sealed 16th October 1958

THE HOUSEHOLD CAVALRY
Sealed 22nd August 1962

THE QUEENS BAY (2ND
DRAGOON GUARDS)
Sealed 14th April 1959

1ST THE QUEENS DRAGOON
GUARDS
Sealed 15th September 1965

3RD CARABINIERS
Sealed 7th October 1963

THE ROYAL SCOTS GREYS
Sealed 28th June 1963

4TH / 7TH ROYAL DRAGOON
GUARDS
Sealed 24th February 1964

THE ROYAL DRAGOONS
Sealed 30th December 1963

THE QUEEN'S OWN HUSSARS
Sealed 15th September 1958

9TH QUEEN'S ROYAL LANCERS
Sealed 9th July 1954

12TH ROYAL LANCERS
Sealed 1st December 1954

11TH HUSSARS
Sealed 6th November 1964

13TH / 18TH ROYAL HUSSARS
Sealed 7th May 1962

14TH / 20TH KING'S HUSSARS
Sealed 28th July 1961

15TH / 19TH THE KING'S ROYAL
HUSSARS
Sealed 8th September 1959

16TH / 5TH QUEEN'S ROYAL
LANCERS
Sealed 25th October 1956

17TH / 21ST LANCERS
Sealed July 1961

ROYAL ARMOURED CORPS
Sealed 20th June 1958

ROYAL CORPS OF SIGNALS
Sealed 31st March 1955

ROYAL HORSE ARTILLERY
Sealed 22nd March 1966

ROYAL ARTILLERY
Sealed 23rd June 1954

ROYAL SIGNALS
Sealed 31st March 1955

GRENADIER GUARDS
Sergeants & Musicians
20th September 1963
o/r's 19th March 1962

COLDSTREAM GUARDS
20th May 1958

SCOTS GUARDS
Colour - Sergt Sergt & Musicians
26th June 1964
o/r 20th May 1958

IRISH GUARDS
20th May 1953

THE QUEEN'S ROYAL REGT
Sealed 18th August 1961

THE BUFFS
Sealed 14th January 1964

THE KING'S OWN ROYAL REGT
Sealed 17th October 1954

THE KING'S REGT
Sealed 22nd November 1971

THE NORFOLK REGT
Sealed 21st April 1964

THE LINCOLNSHIRE REGT
Sealed 11th March 1965

THE LEICESTERSHIRE REGT
Sealed 11th July 1968

ROYAL SCOTS FUS
Sealed 11th July 1957

THE ROYAL WELCH FUS
Sealed 27th April 1962

CHESHIRE REGT
Sealed 26th May 1966

THE SOUTH WALES BORDERERS
Sealed 8th April 1964

THE EAST LANCASHIRE REGT
Sealed 26th May 1966

THE DUKE OF CORNWALL'S
LIGHT INFANTRY
Sealed 4th February 1964

THE DUKE OF WELLINGTON'S
REGT
Sealed 7th April 1970

GLOUCESTERSHIRE REGT
Back Badge
20th March 1967

ROYAL SUSSEX REGT
Sealed 4th May 1954

ROYAL HAMPSHIRE REGT
Sealed 12th May 1971

SOUTH STAFFORDSHIRE REGT
Sealed 21st January 1966

DORSET REGT
Sealed 4th October 1956

SOUTH LANCASHIRE
17th October 1963 Beret Badge
22nd February 1965

WELCH REGT
Sealed 24th August 1964

OXFORDSHIRE &
BUCKINGHAMSHIRE L I
Sealed 28th August 1964

ESSEX REGT
Sealed 1st February 1966

NORTHAMPTONSHIRE REGT
Sealed 6th May 1965

ROYAL WEST KENT REGT
Sealed 2nd November 1964

K.O.Y.L.I.
Sealed 25th April 1951

K.S.L.I.
Sealed 14th August 1963

MIDDLESEX REGT
Sealed 22nd June 1964

WILTSHIRE REGT
PP- 26th August 1964

MANCHESTER REGT
Sealed 24th August 1964

N STAFF REGT
Sealed 26th April 1966

Y&L
1st November 1963

SEAFORTH HIGHLANDERS
Sealed 6th November 1964

CAMERON HIGHLANDERS
Sealed 8th January 1965

ROYAL ULSTER RIFLES
Sealed 28th May 1964

LOWLAND BRIGADE
Sealed 17th November 1958

HOME COUNTIES BRIGADE
Sealed 22nd May 1958

FUSILIER BRIGADE
Sealed 5th September 1958

FORESTER BRIGADE
Sealed 14th April 1959

EAST ANGLIAN BRIGADE
Sealed 22nd May 1958

NORTH IRISH BRIGADE
Sealed 8th December 1958

GREEN JACKETS BRIGADE
Sealed 7th October 1958

QUEEN'S REGT
Sealed 10th July 1966

ROYAL ANGLIAN REGT
Sealed 25th March 1954

GLIDER PILOT REGT
KC Sealed 10th November 1950
QC Sealed 12th October 1955

PARACHUTE REGT
Sealed 18th April 1966

10th GURKHA RIFLES
Beret Officers Sealed 18th October
1961
Beret O/R'S Sealed 30th June 1961

GURKHA ENGINEERS
Sealed 19th November 1958

GURKHA MILITARY POLICE
Sealed 23rd June 1959

R.A.S.C.
QC Sealed 16th August 1961

R.E.M.E.
Sealed 25th September 1963

SMALL ARMS SCHOOL CORPS
Sealed 6th September 1956

ROYAL HOSPITAL CHELSEA
Sealed 11th August 1954

BERKSHIRE YEO
Sealed 8th May 1952
Beret Sealed 8th May 1952

QUEEN'S OWN YEO
Sealed 29th March 1972

NORTHUMBERLAND FUS
KC Sealed 17th September 1951
QC Sealed 13th March 1962

YORKSHIRE YEO
Sealed 20th April 1960

EAST RIDING YEO
Sealed 11th March 1952

AYRSHIRE YEO
Smaller (of) Word
Sealed 30th April 1965

CHESHIRE YEO
Sealed 19th February 1963

ROYAL DEVON YEO ARTY
KC Sealed 21st February 1952
QC Sealed 22nd June 1956

WORCESTERSHIRE HUSSARS
Sealed 16th November 1951

STAFFORDSHIRE YEO
KC 8th August 1952

SHROPSHIRE YEO
KC 24th November 1950
QC 8th April 1957

LANCASTER YEO
Sealed 17th September 1951

LOTHIANS & BORDER HORSE
Sealed 11th January 1962

HIGHLAND YEO
Sealed 7th April 1960

SCOTTISH HORSE
Sealed 30th October 1951

INNS OF COURT REGT
Sealed 13th November 1958

CITY OF LONDON YEO
Sealed 3rd April 1959

SUSSEX YEO
KC Sealed 5th May 1952
QC Sealed 8th January 1957

HERTFORDSHIRE YEO
Sealed 21st May 1955

LOYAL SUFFOLK HUSSARS
Beret 14th September 1953

NORFOLK YEO
Sealed 17th October 1953

ESSEX YEO
KC Beret Sealed 17th June 1952
QC Beret Sealed 30th August 1957

LOVAT SCOUTS
Square Lettering To Motto
Sealed 10th January 1951
Tall Lettering To Motto
Sealed 21st September 1965

SURREY YEO
Sealed 24th January 1958
Smaller 28th January 1958

LEICESTERSHIRE &
DERBYSHIRE
Sealed 14th March 1957

ROYAL BUCKINGHAMSHIRE
HUSSARS
Sealed 22nd February 1952

CAERNARVON & DENBIGH YEO
Sealed 28th January 1952

FLINT & DENBIGH YEO
Sealed 28th January 1958

SOUTH NOTTINGHAMSHIRE
HUSSARS
Sealed 14th February 1952

NORTH SOMERSET YEO
Sealed 18th November 1958

OXFORDSHIRE HUSSARS
Sealed 9th May 1952

BEDFORDSHIRE REGT
Sealed 1st January 1960

GLASGOW HIGHLANDER
Sealed 19th February 1957

13TH LONDON
Sealed 13th March 1953

14TH LONDON
Sealed 27th June 1964

18TH LONDON
Sealed 6th March 1957

23RD LONDON
Sealed 28th January 1958

BIRMINGHAM UNIVERSITY
Sealed 24th August 1950

MANCHESTER UNIVERSITY
O.T.C
Sealed 18th July 1950

ST ANDREWS UNI U.T.C
Sealed 26th January 1951

UNIVERSITY OF WALES U.T.C
Sealed 24th August 1950

QUEEN VICTORIA SCHOOL
DUNBLANE
Sealed 7th December 1964

ROYAL DRAGOON GUARDS
Sealed 2nd September 1992
NCO 2nd September 1992

KING'S ROYAL HUSSARS
Sealed 22nd February 1995

LIGHT DRAGOONS
SIL/GOLD 18th January 1993
SIL/GOLD BLUE ENAMEL
25th February 1995

QUEEN'S ROYAL LANCERS
Sealed 14th July 1961

ROYAL IRISH REGT
Sealed 11th June 1993

ROYAL PIONEER CORPS
Sealed 25th February 1985

ADJUTANT GENERALS CORPS
50mm 15th June 1992
45mm 16th February 1994